NOUR ELLEUCH
Sonda Jardak
Aya Hammami

Non-invasive methods of fibrosis in chronic hepatitis B

NOUR ELLEUCH
Sonda Jardak
Aya Hammami

Non-invasive methods of fibrosis in chronic hepatitis B

Evaluation of non-invasive methods for fibrosis hepatic in chronic hepatitis B in a Tunisian population

ScienciaScripts

Imprint

Cover image: www.ingimage.com

This book is a translation from the original published under ISBN 978-3-330-86932-5.

Publisher:
Sciencia Scripts
is a trademark of
Dodo Books Indian Ocean Ltd., member of the OmniScriptum S.R.L Publishing group
str. A.Russo 15, of. 61, Chisinau-2068, Republic of Moldova Europe
Printed at: see last page
ISBN: 978-620-0-87117-6

Non-invasive methods of fibrosis in chronic hepatitis B

Table of Contents

Acknowledgements

I dedicate this memoir to

To my dear daddy:

Taieb

Who has constantly supported and encouraged me throughout my journey, I offer you this work as a token of all the affection and gratitude I have for you.

In memory of my mom:

Mounira

I so wish I could have seen you by my side and seen you proud of what I've become. May your soul rest in peace my dear and only mother.

To my mother-in-law Nedia:

I thank you for your gentleness, tenderness and generosity. I dedicate this work to you as an expression of my total respect and admiration.

To my dearest husband Majed:

No dedication could possibly express how much I feel for you. Thank you for always being at my side, by your presence, by your devoted love and your tenderness.

To my in-laws:

Mohamed and Moufida

Please perceive through this work, the expression of my deep affection and enormous respect.

To my dear sister Sonia

No matter what I say, I cannot express the love and tenderness I have for you. I'll never forget all the sacrifices you've made for me.

To my brother Tarak, his wife Mariem and their angels Malek and Yassin:

May God protect your in-laws. I wish you happiness.

To my brother-in-law Malek, his wife Ameni and their daughters Fatma and Emna:

Please perceive through this work, the expression of my deep affection and enormous respect. With all the love I have for you, I wish you much happiness in your life.

To my teacher and president of the jury Mrs. Professor Asma Ouakaa

You do me the honor of agreeing to chair my memoir jury. Please find, through this work, the testimony of my gratitude and my deep respect.

To my master and judge Associate Professor Rim Neifar

You honor me with your trust by agreeing to judge this work. Please accept my deep respect and thanks. Your presence will be a pleasure and a tremendous support

To my master and judge Madam Associate Professor Norsaf Bibani

You honor me by accepting my invitation to serve on this jury. Please accept my deep respect and thanks for the honour you do me by agreeing to judge this work.

To my memory director, Mrs. Nour Elleuch University Hospital Assistant

Your help in the elaboration of this work, your availability, your eternal good mood and your patience touched me enormously. May success, happiness and health accompany you throughout your personal and professional life.

Introduction

Assessment of the severity of liver damage, which determines both prognosis and therapeutic indications, is of paramount importance in chronic hepatitis B [1]. Two objectives are important in clinical practice: the detection of significant fibrosis and the detection of cirrhosis [2]. Until now, the assessment of the severity of fibrosis has been based on liver biopsy puncture (PBF). The limitations of PBF (invasiveness, sampling bias and inter-observer variability) have led to the development of alternative non-invasive methods [3]. These are essentially based on two types of approaches: serum fibrosis scores (specific or not for hepatitis B) and measurement of liver elasticity by pulse elastometry (EI) [1].

Hepatic elastometry is currently validated by the scientific societies as a non-invasive method for assessing fibrosis in chronic hepatitis B [4].

In Tunisia, to date, there are no studies evaluating the concordance between the different non-invasive markers of fibrosis and the histological score of fibrosis in patients with chronic hepatitis B.

The main objective of our study was to evaluate the correlation between hepatic elasticity and the histological score of fibrosis in Tunisian patients with chronic hepatitis B.

The secondary objective of this study was to compare the diagnostic performance of different non-invasive markers of fibrosis to predict significant and severe fibrosis in chronic hepatitis B.

Patients and methods

1. **Type of study :**

This was an analytical prospective study, spread over a period of 3 years from January 2015 to December 2017, carried out at the gastroenterology department of the Sahloul University Hospital Centre in Sousse on patients being followed for chronic hepatitis B.

1.1 Criteria for inclusion :

We included patients older than 18 years of age, with chronic hepatitis B defined by HBs antigen carrying for more than 6 months associated with a viral load ≥ 2000 IU/ml and/or higher than normal alanine aminotransferase (ALAT) levels.

1.2 Criteria for non-inclusion :

Patients were not included in this study:

- Having clinico-biological, endoscopic and/or radiological signs of cirrhosis.
- Having viral co-infection with hepatitis C virus, delta virus or human immunodeficiency virus.
- Having hepatocellular carcinoma.
- Having an alcohol consumption ≥20g g/d for women and ≥30 g/d for men.
- With prior antiviral B therapy.
- Not meeting the criteria for validity of the fibroscan result.
- Presenting fibroscan failure factors: obesity with a IMC≥30 kg/m^2, ascites [5].
- Confounding factors that may increase elasticity values independently of fibrosis are cytolysis >5N, extrahepatic cholestasis, congestive heart failure and excessive alcohol intake [5].
- Having a contraindication to PBF.

1.3 EXCLUSION CRITERION

Patients wishing to terminate their participation were excluded.

2. Methods :

2.1. Data collection :

For all patients included, we found the following data:

2.1.1. Sociodemographic and anamnestic data :

- Age.
- Sex.
- Weight in kg, height in m and body mass index in kg/m2(BMI). Overweight is defined by a BMI ≥25 Kg/m².
- Tobacco consumption quantified in packages year.
- Alcohol consumption (absentee, occasional, excessive withdrawal). Average consumption was quantified (in grams of alcohol per day).
- Comorbidities (hypertension, diabetes, dyslipidemia).

2.1.2. Biological data :

- Blood counts: leukocytes, hemoglobinemia, platelets, etc.
- Liver workup: ALAT [VN < 40UI/L] and aspartate amino transferase (ASAT) [VN < 37UI/L], gammaglutamyl transferase (GGT) [VN < 35UI/L], alkaline phosphatases (PAL) [VN=64 - 306UI/L], total [VN<17µmol/L] and conjugated bilirubinemia, prothrombin (TP) and INR (International Normalized Ratio) levels.
- Complete serology for hepatitis B virus (HBV) (HBsAg, HBeAg and HBe antibodies)
- The HBV viral load expressed in IU/l.

2.2 Assessment of fibrosis :

2.2.1. Non-invasive markers of fibrosis

2.2.1.1. Serum tests:

The biological parameters measured allowed the calculation of the following non-invasive scores:

- APRI (aspartate aminotransferase to platelet ratio index) score [6] :

An APRI score ≤0.5 corresponded to minimal fibrosis; a score ≥1.5 corresponded to cirrhosis.

- FIB- 4 score (Fibro index 4) [7] :

An FIB-4≤ score of 1.45 corresponded to minimal fibrosis; a ≥ score of 3.25 corresponded to cirrhosis.

- The GPR (Gama-glutamyltransferase to platelet ratio index) score [8]:

A GPR < 0.32 was indicative of minimal fibrosis, while a GPR > 0.56 was indicative of cirrhosis [8].

The formulas for the different scores are summarized in Table I :

Table I : Formulas for calculating the different non-invasive fibrosis scores

Score	**Formula to calculate the score**
APRI Score	ASAT (/LSN) x 100 / inserts
Score FIB-4	(Age x ASAT) / (pads x ALAT1/2)
GPR Score	(GGT/LSN)/platelets] × 100

2.2.1.2. Impulse Elastometry: Fibroscan

All patients were given a "Echosens model 402" fibroscan with a Ms probe according to a standardized protocol. This was performed after a fasting period of at least 2 hours. The examination was carried out in a patient in supine position, with the right arm under the head in maximum abduction to free the right hypochondrium. After application of gel to the skin, the probe was positioned by the operator perpendicular to the skin at the level of the right lobe of the liver. A minimum of 10 valid measurements were taken for each patient. Liver elasticity was expressed in kiloPascals (kPa) and was the median of 10 valid measurements. The median value is considered valid under 2 conditions:

- An interquartile range (IQR) value (assessing the variability of valid measurements) less than 30% of the median [5].
- A success rate (number of valid measurements compared to the number of measurements performed) greater than 60% [5].

The time interval between the completion of the AE and the PBF was less than 3 months.

2.2.2. Liver puncture biopsy :

All patients had a PBF after information and consent, and in the absence of contraindications.

A haemostasis check-up less than a week old and an abdominal ultrasound less than 6 months old were systematically performed.

The PBF was performed transparietally under local anaesthesia using a modified Menghini-type needle (Hepafix) of 1.6mm gauge. The sample was packed in 10% buffered formalin and analysed by an experienced pathologist who was unaware of the results of the non-invasive tests.

The assessment of the severity of necrotico-inflammatory lesions and the stage of fibrosis was based on the Metavir score. It takes into account the necrotico-inflammatory activity of hepatitis according to a score (A) between 0 and 3 and the degree of severity of fibrosis according to a score (F) between 0 and 4 (Table II).

Table II: Metavir Score

F0	Absence of fibrosis	**A0**	Lack of histological activity
F1	Portal and periportal fibrosis without fibrous septa	**A1**	Minimal histological activity
F2	Portal and periportal fibrosis with rare fibrous septa	**A2**	Moderate histological activity
F3	Portal and periportal fibrosis with numerous fibrous septa	**A3**	Severe histological activity
F4	Cirrhosis		

Fibrosis is considered to be:

- Absent or minimal for a stage of fibrosis (F0, F1).
- Significant for a stage of fibrosis ≥ F2.
- Severe for a stage of fibrosis ≥ F3.

2.3. Statistical analysis :

The data entry was performed using SPSS version 20 software and consisted of two components: the first descriptive and the second analytical.

2.3.1. Descriptive study

Quantitative variables were expressed as mean ± standard deviation.

Simple and relative frequencies were calculated for the qualitative variables.

2.3.2. Analytical study :

The diagnostic performance of each of the fibrosis markers was analyzed using the Pearson Correlation Test and the receiver operating curve (ROC) to compare them.

The diagnostic values of the scores were calculated using the usual informational indices: sensitivity, specificity, positive (VPP) and negative (VPN) predictive values and Receiver operating characteristic (ROC) curves. The areas under the ROC curves (AUROCs) were calculated for each fibrosis marker by the non-parametric empirical method of De Long et al.

The cut-off value for the prediction of significant fibrosis was chosen from the ROC curve. It corresponds to the value for which sensitivity and specificity are maximal.

The percentage of biopsies avoided corresponds to the number of patients correctly classified for each threshold out of the total number of patients.

A p-value<0,05 was considered significant.

2.4. Ethical considerations :

This work did not present any conflict of interest. Strict anonymity and confidentiality of the individual data collected were respected throughout the study.

Results

1. Study population :

During the study period, 102 patients with chronic hepatopathy B were monitored in the department. Fifty-five patients were not included because they were already in the cirrhosis stage (49 patients), had HCC (9 patients). Four patients were excluded. In the end, our study included 43 patients.

2. Descriptive study of the study population :

2.1. General patient characteristics :

In total, we included 43 patients.

2.1.1. Age:

The mean age of the patients was 38 years (±10.05) with extremes ranging from 20 to 65 years.

2.1.2. Sex:

The patients were divided into 23 men and 20 women. The sex ratio of males to females was 1.1.

2.1.3. BMI:

The average BMI was 22.86 kg/m² [19 - 29 kg/m²]. Ten patients (23%) were overweight.

2.1.4. Life habits:

Smoking was found in 19 patients (44.1%) with an average consumption of 21 packet years.

Occasional or current excessive alcohol consumption was noted in respectively 10 patients (23.2%) and 2 patients (4.6%) with an average daily alcohol consumption of 30 g/d.

2.1.5. Comorbidities:

A history of diabetes, dyslipidemia or hypertension was present in 6 (13.9%), 4 (9.3%) and 6 (13.9%) patients, respectively.

2.2 Biological characteristics :

Cytolysis was found in 9 patients (20.9%) with a mean transaminase value of 48.65 IU/L ±16.36 IU/L for AST and 48.79 IU/L ±19.59 IU/L for ALT.

Seven patients had viral loads <2000 IU/ml.

Eight patients (18.6%) had a viral load ≥ at 2000 IU/ml and cytolysis.

Thirty-five patients (81.3%) were HBe antigen negative.

Table III reports the different biological parameters of the study population.

Table III: Biological parameters of the study population

	Average value ± standard deviation (or median)	Extreme values
Viral load B (IU/ml)	3132521.87 IU/ml ± 17209910	[20-110000000]
Brochures (10^3 elements/mm^3)	203,11±58,72	[97-365]
ASAT (IU/l)	38,65±16,36	[19-80]
ALAT (IU/l)	38,79 ±19,59	[3-120]
Total bilirubinemia (µmol/l)	11,08±4,38	[5-21]
PAL (IU/l)	101±39,16	[8-230]
GGT (IU/l)	35,39±17,57	[3-88]
TP (%)	90	[71-100]
Albuminemia (g/l)	36,11±2,48	[26-42]

2.3 Assessment of fibrosis :

2.3.1. Results of the PBF :

PBF was performed after clinical and ultrasound identification of the liver in 38 (88.3%) and 5 (11.7%) patients, respectively. The mean length of the liver core was 16.34 ± 0.85 mm [4- 45] and the mean number of portal spaces was 10.7 ± 3.66 [2-17].

Patients were divided into 3 categories according to the stage of fibrosis:

- Minimal or absent fibrosis (F0-F1): 30 patients.
- Significant Fibrosis (F2-F3): 13 patients.
- Severe fibrosis (F3-F4): 3 patients.

The histological analysis by Metavir score is summarized in Table IV.

Table IV: PBF results

	Stadium	Number of employees N(%)
Necrotico-inflammatory activity (METAVIR)	A0	3 (7%)
	A1	28 (65,1%)
	A2	10 (23,3%)
	A3	2 (4,7%)
The stage of fibrosis (METAVIR)	F0	8 (18,6%)
	F1	22 (51,2%)
	F2	10 (23,3%)
	F3	3 (7%)
	F4	0 (0%)

2.3.2. Non-invasive markers of fibrosis :

2.3.2.1. Pulse elastometry :

The AR was performed in the same week as the PBF in 22 patients (51.1%) and in the same month in 15 others (34.8%). Six patients (13.9%) had both examinations within a longer time frame (46 days) but less than 90 days.

The mean value of the valid measurements was 13. The mean RDI/median value and the mean success rate were 15.4% [3-30%] and 80% [60-100%], respectively.

The mean value of hepatic elasticity was 6.19±3.16 kPa with extremes ranging from 2.8 to 11.3 kPa.

Liver elasticity values as a function of stage of fibrosis are shown in Table V.

Table V: Liver elasticity in kPa as a function of stage of fibrosis

	N (%)	Average	Minimum	Maximum
F0	8 (18,6%)	3,7	3,5	5,8
F1	22 (51,2%)	5,2	2,8	8,1
F2	10 (23,3%)	6,4	3,3	8,2
F3	3 (6,9%)	12,6	8,9	11,3
F4	0			
F0-F1	30 (69,7%)	4,45	2,8	8,1
F2-F3	13 (30,2%)	9,5	3,7	17,3

2.3.2.2. Serum tests :

The mean value of the APRI score was 0.54 with extremes ranging from 0.17 to 1.89.

The mean values of the FIB 4 and GPR scores were 1.31 [0.4-3.18] and 0.58 [0.03-1.89], respectively.

According to the APRI score, no patient had minimal fibrosis and 2 patients were considered cirrhotic.

According to FIB 4 scores, 30 patients (69.7%) had minimal fibrosis and no patients had cirrhosis.

According to the GPR score, fibrosis was considered minimal in 9 patients (20.9%) and severe in 12 patients (27.9%).

The distribution of patients by degree of fibrosis as assessed by non-invasive markers of fibrosis are listed in Table VI.

Table VI: Distribution of Patients by Degree of Fibrosis as Measured by the Different Non-invasive Markers of Fibrosis

	Average value	**Minimal Fibrosis N(%)**	**Significant Fibrosis N(%)**	**Severe Fibrosis N(%)**
Fibroscan (KPa)	6,19	30 (69,7%)	13 (30,2%)	3 (6,9%)
APRI	0,54	0 (0%)	41 (95,3%)	2 (4,6%)
FIB4	1,31	30 (69,7%)	13 (30,3%)	0 (0%)
GPR	0,58	9 (20,9%)	22 (51,2%)	12 (27,9%)

Minimal fibrosis (F0-F1), significant fibrosis (≥F2), severe fibrosis (≥F4)

3. Analytical study :

3.1 Correlation between liver elasticity and histological fibrosis score :

3.1.1. Significant fibrosis :

A statistically significant correlation was found between liver elasticity and fibrosis severity ($r = 0.50$, $p=0.001$).

Thirty-three patients (76.7%) had a good agreement between liver elasticity and stage of fibrosis according to the Metavir score. Ten patients (23.2%) had a discrepancy: 3 patients had liver elasticity ≤ 6.5 kPa and fibrosis ≥ F2 according to the Metavir score and the remaining 7 patients had liver elasticity > 6.5 kPa and fibrosis < F2 according to the Metavir score.

Liver biopsies were avoided in 35 patients (81.3%).

The AUROC for the detection of significant fibrosis (METAVIR F≥2) was 0.76 (95% CI = 0.60-0.93), with a p=0.005 (Figure 1). The cut-off value for hepatic elasticity predicting significant fibrosis was 6.5 kPa with a sensitivity of 76%, specificity of 76%, PPV of 65.5% and NPV of 83.3%.

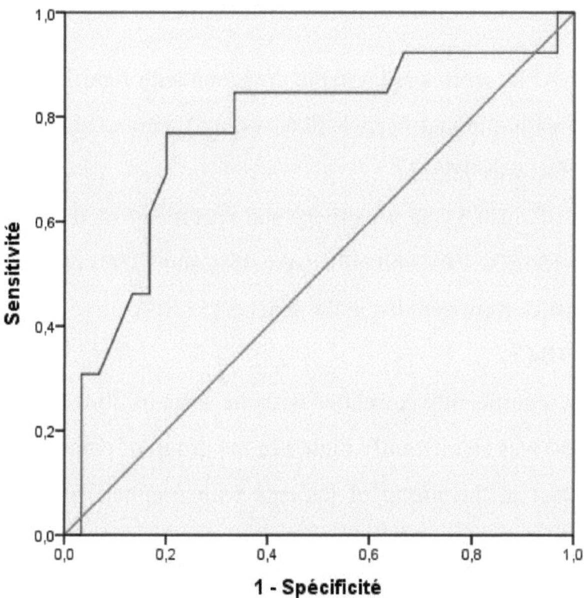

Figure 1: ROC curve for the detection of significant fibrosis by fibroscan

3.1.2. Severe fibrosis :

The analytical statistical study was not performed only for the prediction of severe fibrosis due to the small size of this population (N=3). Taking as a threshold for the diagnosis of severe fibrosis the value of 9 KPa in the absence of cytolysis and 12 KPa in the presence of ALAT>5, 2 patients/3 (66.6%) were correctly classified by the fibroscan.

3.2. Diagnostic performance of serum fibrosis tests in chronic hepatitis B

3.2.1. Significant fibrosis :

3.2.1.1. APRI :

The APRI score was not significantly correlated with the stage of fibrosis (p=0.3).

The mean APRI score was higher in the group with significant fibrosis than in the group with minimal fibrosis (0.64 vs. 0.5) with no significant difference. The AUROC was 0.58.

For a cut-off of 0.5, the sensitivity and specificity of the APRI score were 53.8% and 56.6%. PPV and NPV were 35% and 73.9% respectively.

Liver biopsies were avoided in 24 patients (55.8%).

3.2.1.2. FIB4 :

FIB 4 was significantly correlated with the stage of fibrosis with p=0.04.

Mean FIB4 was significantly higher in the group of patients with significant fibrosis than in the group of patients with minimal fibrosis (1.7 vs. 0.6; p=0.03). AUROC was 0.74.

For a cut-off value of 1.45, FIB 4 had a sensitivity of 61.5% and a specificity of 83.3%. PPV and NPV were 61.5% and 83.3%.

Liver biopsies were avoided in 33 patients (76.7%).

3.2.1.3. GPR :

The GPR score was not significantly correlated with the stage of fibrosis (p=0.4).

The mean GPR was higher in the group with significant fibrosis than in the group with minimal fibrosis (0.63 vs. 0.56) with no significant difference. The AUROC was 0.54.

Using a cut-off of 0.32, the GPR score had a sensitivity of 84.6% and a specificity of 23.3%. PPV and NPV were 32.3% and 77.7% respectively.

Liver biopsies were avoided in 18 patients (41.8%).

Table VII summarizes the diagnostic performance of each of the non-invasive fibrosis tests.

Table VII: Diagnostic performance of non-invasive fibrosis tests.

	≥ F2					
Test	Cut-Off	AUROC	Sensitivity (%)	V PP (%)	VPN (%)	Specificity (%)
GPR	0,32	0,54	84,6	23,3	32,3	77,7
APRI	0,5	0,58	53,8	56,6	35	73,9
FIB4	1,45	0,74	61	83,3	61,5	83,3
EI	6,5	0,76	76	76 65,5	83,3	

3.2.2. Severe fibrosis:

The analytical statistical study was not carried out only for the prediction of severe fibrosis due to the small size of this population.

3.3 Overall comparison of diagnostic performance of non-invasive scores in the assessment of significant fibrosis:

Among the non-invasive scores studied, AE and FIB4 were correlated with significant fibrosis as shown by the ROC curve with AUROCs of 0.76 and 0.74 respectively (Figure 2).

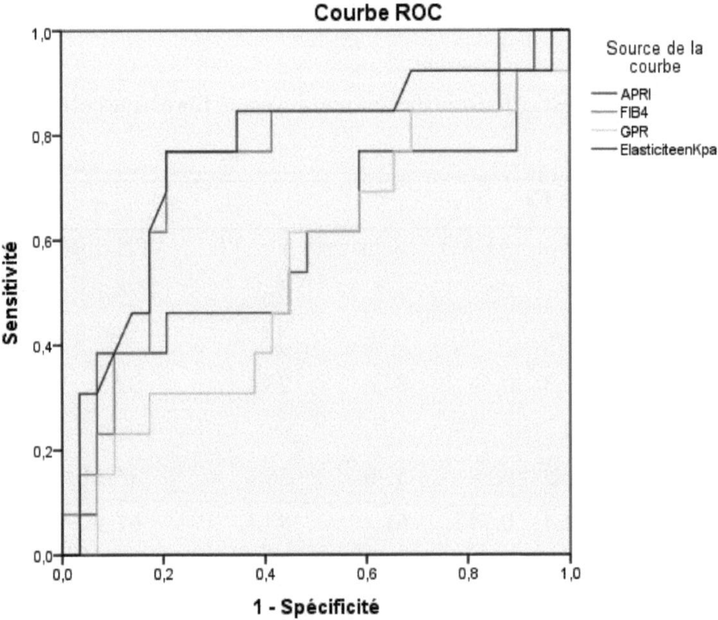

Figure 2: ROC curves for the detection of significant fibrosis by non-invasive tests

For a threshold of 6.5 KPa, the AR had the best sensitivity (76%). For a threshold of 1.45, FIB 4 had the best specificity (83.3%). These 2 methods had the best NPVs (83.3%).

At the thresholds of 6.5 KPa for AR, 1.45 for FIB4; 0.5 for APRI score and 0.32 for GPR, liver biopsies were avoided in 35 (81.3%), 33(76.7%); 24(55.8%) and 18 (41.8%) patients respectively.

Discussion

In our study, 30 patients had minimal or absent fibrosis, 13 patients had significant fibrosis, of which 3 had severe fibrosis.

AEs and FIB4 were correlated with significant fibrosis with AUROCs of 0.76 and 0.74 respectively. At the 6.5 KPa thresholds for AE, 1.45 for FIB4 liver biopsies were avoidable in 35 (81.3%) and 33 (76.7%) patients respectively.

The discussion will be organized in 6 parts. The first part will focus on the role of PBF in the assessment of fibrosis in chronic hepatitis B. The second part will focus on the place of AR in this fibrosis assessment. The third part will be dedicated to the place of serum scores and the fourth part will be devoted to the comparison of different non-invasive markers of fibrosis. The fifth part will draw up recommendations. Finally, the sixth part will highlight the strengths and limitations of this work.

1. Place of liver puncture biopsy in the assessment of fibrosis :

The PBF, which allows an anatomo-pathological examination of the collected liver, is the reference examination to assess the degree and distribution of the main liver lesions, particularly necrotico-inflammatory activity and fibrosis. However, PBF remains an invasive procedure with a morbidity risk of 0.3% to 0.6% and a mortality risk of 0 to 0.05% [9]. Another limitation of PBF is the sampling problem. Indeed, there is a difference in the fibrosis score of at least one stage between right and left liver biopsies in 33% of patients with chronic hepatitis C [10].

On the other hand, liver histology does not allow us to appreciate the "dynamics" of the fibrosis process. All these data justify the search for new non-invasive markers of fibrosis. These tests are considered to be effective if they differentiate between patients with significant fibrosis and those with minimal or absent fibrosis, and also between those with cirrhosis and those without cirrhosis [3].

2. Place of pulse elastometry in the evaluation of fibrosis :

In our study, with respect to AEs, we found an AUROC for the detection of significant fibrosis at 0.76. This defines this method as moderately informative in our patients to determine significant fibrosis ≥ F2. This is the case in almost all studies that have compared liver elasticity with histology in the evaluation of fibrosis during chronic viral hepatitis B. Chon's meta-analysis, published in 2012, included 18 controlled studies evaluating the diagnostic performance of fibroscan compared to PBF, with a total of 2772 patients with chronic hepatitis B. This meta-analysis reported an AUROC of 0.859 calculated from the AUROC values of 10 studies [11].

In our study, the cut-off value, which distinguishes significant fibrosis from minimal or even absent fibrosis, was 6.5KPa with a sensitivity and specificity of 76%. This threshold value varies between studies. In Chon's meta-analysis, the cut-off was 7.9 KPa with extremes ranging from 6.1 to 11.8 kPa [11]. This variability in the cut-off value currently poses the problem of a universal reference for characterizing patients.

Similarly, sensitivity and specificity vary between studies. They were 74.3% and 78.3% respectively in Cohn's meta-analysis [11].

In our series, the PPV of the AE was average (65.5%) while the NPV was good (83.3%). These values also vary widely between studies: a meta-analysis including 79 studies reported a 74% PPV (69-78) and 84% higher NPV (80-87) [12].

In our study, 2 out of 3 patients with severe fibrosis were correctly classified by AR. In the literature, several studies and meta-analyses have confirmed that AEs perform better for the diagnosis of cirrhosis than for the diagnosis of significant fibrosis and were better at ruling out cirrhosis than at affirming it, with an NPV of around 96% versus 74% PPV [13].

3. Place of serum tests in the evaluation of fibrosis:

➢ FIB 4:

In our study, FIB4 was the best performing serum marker for the diagnosis of significant fibrosis with an AUROC of 0.74, elevated NPV (83.3%) and good sensitivity (61.5%).
In the meta-analysis of Xiao et al published in 2014, the AUROC value for FIB4 was 0.78 for significant fibrosis, 0.82 for severe fibrosis and 0.84 for cirrhosis [14].
For a cut-off of 1.45, sensitivity was 65.4% and specificity 73.6% with a PPV of 76.2% and a NPV of 81.4% [14].
The study by Mallet et al, found that the FIB-4 score was more accurate than the APRI score to exclude severe fibrosis with an 86% NPV for a FIB-4 score ≤ 1.45 (even better for a value <0.7) while for values >1.45 its performance remains limited and unsatisfactory [15].

➢ The APRI score

Although the APRI has been recommended as a "perfect non-invasive model" for assessing hepatic fibrosis by the Asia Pacific Association for the Study of the Liver (APASL) and the WHO Chronic Hepatitis B guidelines [16, 17]; several other studies have concluded that the APRI score has only moderate sensitivity and accuracy for assessing fibrosis during chronic hepatitis B. Indeed, in the study by Wai et al published in 2006, the APRI score was less effective in detecting significant fibrosis (AUROC=0.63) and cirrhosis (AUROC=0.64) than in hepatitis C [18]. These results were confirmed in the meta-analysis of Xiao et al which showed that the performance of the APRI score was average for the assessment of fibrosis. With thresholds of 0.5, 1.0 and 1.5, the sensitivity and specificity values of the APRI score were 70% and

60%, 50% and 83% respectively, and 36.9% and 92.5% for significant fibrosis, advanced fibrosis and cirrhosis [14]. Using a threshold of 0.5 for significant fibrosis, the PPV and NPV of the APRI score were 61.7% and 52.9% respectively [14]. These results are similar to our study: AUROC for the diagnosis of significant fibrosis at 0.58 with PPV and NPV of 35% and 73.9%.

➢ **The GPR:**

In our study, GPR was the least effective non-invasive test for the diagnosis of significant fibrosis (AUROC =0.54).

Using a cut-off of 0.32, the GPR score had a sensitivity of 84.6% and a specificity of 23.3%. PPV and NPV were 32.3% and 77.7% respectively.

Lemoine et al, who developed this index, reported in their work that GPR was more effective in diagnosing significant fibrosis thanFIB4 and the APRI score in the black African population (AUROC for GPR=0.8 vs 0.66 for APRI and FIB4). For a cut-off of 0.32, the sensitivity and specificity of GPR were 83% and 69% respectively (19). In the French population, the performance of GPR was equivalent to that of FIB4 and the APRI score (AUROC=0.72) [19].

In a meta-analysis published in 2019 including 10 studies with a total of 5882 patients, the GPR score was moderately good for the diagnosis of significant fibrosis (AUROC=0.73) [20].

4. Comparison of non-invasive means of fibrosis :

Little work has been done to directly compare these different non-invasive means of fibrosis during chronic viral hepatitis B. Some studies have concluded that GPR is superior to FIB4 and APRI scores in the diagnosis of fibrosis [20,21]. Another study reported that FIB4 was more accurate than the APRI score in excluding severe fibrosis but not reliable for the diagnosis of cirrhosis [15]. Comparing the performance of serum tests with that of the AE, the results were more consistent: AE and serum tests have similar diagnostic performance for the diagnosis of significant fibrosis [5]. On the other hand,

AE has superior diagnostic performance to serum tests for the diagnosis of advanced fibrosis or cirrhosis [22], including excellent NPV (>90%) [23].

For this reason, in its 2014 report evaluating non-invasive methods for the measurement of fibrosis in untreated chronic hepatitis B, the HAS recommends the use of AR for the diagnosis of cirrhosis, if cirrhosis is not evident [2].

5. **Recommendations**

The EASL and the ALEH jointly issued recommendations in 2015 validating the use of AR in the pre-therapeutic evaluation of chronic viral hepatitis B. An elasticity value < 6 kPa eliminates significant fibrosis and indicates surveillance. A value > 9 kPa (if transaminases are normal) and > 12 KPa (if ALTs are moderately elevated (< 5N)) is associated with a high probability of advanced fibrosis (PPV > 90%) requiring antiviral therapy, screening for esophageal varices and HCC. Between these two thresholds (grey zone), an FBP is recommended if the results influence patient management [5].

However, IE has some drawbacks: high cost, the need for maintenance operations (regular servicing/calibration), qualified operators, and lack of availability in all centres. In addition, AR has low diagnostic accuracy in cases of obesity, moderate or severe necroinflammation, right heart failure and food consumption [17].

These limits leave room for serum testing. These are readily available in low- and middle-income countries, as we are, easy to interpret without special expertise. They can also be performed on an outpatient basis [17].

According to the European recommendations published in 2017, the evaluation of hepatic fibrosis as part of the pre-therapeutic assessment of chronic hepatitis B can be done by both AE and serum tests, but with a preference for fibroscan, the latter being the best studied and having a better performance for the diagnosis of cirrhosis [4].

The WHO Chronic Hepatitis B guidelines have identified IE (where resources permit) and the APRI as the most appropriate tests for the diagnosis of cirrhosis in low- and middle-income countries (such as ours), but draw attention to the low PPV of all non-invasive fibrosis tests for the detection of significant and severe fibrosis, particularly the APRI [17]. In addition, a number of factors need to be considered for correct interpretation of serum tests. Indeed, young age may lead to underestimation of significant fibrosis by the FIB4 and the APRI score [24]. Alcohol abuse (alcoholic hepatitis raises the AST), conditions such as malaria or HIV (which lower platelet counts), or the use of traditional medicines and herbs can also amplify the APRI score [17]. Even moderate increases in ALT levels would reduce the diagnostic performance of both FIB4 and GPR and APRI scores [25].

6. Limitations and strengths of the study

The main limitation of this study is its monocentricity, which considerably reduces the number of patients and therefore the power of the results. Another limitation is the use of a single cut-off value for serum tests which could produce sub-optimal sensitivity and specificity values.

In this case, our study has several assets. It is a study that involved a homogeneous population with very strict inclusion and exclusion criteria. On the other hand, our study was interested in a subject that has been little studied, particularly in Tunisia, and which remains the source of many questions until now.

Conclusions

Assessment of the degree of liver fibrosis is an essential element in establishing the prognosis and for the indication of antiviral treatment. PBF has long been considered the gold standard for the assessment of liver fibrosis and activity. However, it remains an invasive test with certain limitations. Non-invasive tests represent a revolution in the management of chronic hepatitis, in particular by challenging the "gold standard" status of the PBF.

The aim of this work was to evaluate and compare the diagnostic performance of different non-invasive fibrosis markers (EI, FIB4, APRI and GPR) for predicting significant fibrosis during chronic hepatitis B in a Tunisian population, based on a comparison with histological data from liver biopsy.

To do this, we conducted a prospective study involving 43 patients with an average age of 38 years.

Based on histological analysis by Metavir score, 30 patients had absent or minimal fibrosis, 13 patients had significant fibrosis and 3 patients had severe fibrosis.

Among the non-invasive methods studied, only AE and FIB4 were correlated with significant fibrosis (p=0.001 and 0.04 respectively). These 2 methods appeared to be reliable for the detection of significant fibrosis (AUROC of 0.76 and 0.74 respectively).

For a threshold of 6.5 KPa, the AR had the best sensitivity (76%). For a threshold of 1.45, FIB 4 had the best specificity (83.3%). These 2 methods had the best NPVs (83.3%). The AE and FIB4 would thus avoid liver biopsies in 81.3% and 76.7% of patients respectively.

The APRI score and FIB 4 were not good markers to predict significant fibrosis (AUROC 0.58 and 0.54) respectively. Using a cut-off of 0.5 for the APRI score and 0.32 for the GPR, these markers had a low PPV35% and 32.3% respectively. They would, however, avoid liver biopsies in 24 (55.8%) and 18 (41.8%) patients respectively.

For the diagnosis of severe fibrosis, using a threshold value of 9 KPa in the absence of cytolysis and 12 KPa in the presence of ALT>5, 2 patients/3 were correctly classified by the AE. While 1 patient/3 was correctly classified by serum markers using cut-off values of 0.56 for GPR; 1.5 for APRI score and 3.25 for FIB4.

Our study confirms the place of AR in the evaluation of fibrosis in chronic viral hepatitis B, which has been clearly validated in the latest international recommendations.

For serum markers, our results were rather inconsistent with the literature regarding the diagnostic performance of GPR and APRI score. This supports the fact that these serum markers, although simple and inexpensive, do not have sufficient diagnostic performance to assess the stage of fibrosis in any circumstance on their own. Indeed, they may be biased by intercurrent disease or physiological parameters (age) that may falsely increase or decrease scores and thus compromise an objective assessment of fibrosis in chronic hepatitis B.

References

1. Touré PS, Berthé A, Diop MM, Diarra AS, Lô G, Sow-Sall A et al. Non-invasive markers in the evaluation of hepatic fibrosis in Senegalese chronic carriers of the hepatitis B virus: about 404 cases. RAFMI 2017; 4 (2): 30-34.

2. High Authority of Health. Evaluation of non-invasive methods for measuring hepatic fibrosis in chronic hepatitis B. Technological evaluation report. Paris: HAS; 2014.

3. Diallo I, Mbaye PS, Vray M, Ndiaye B, Diop Y, Simon F et al. Evaluation of fibrosis in chronic viral hepatitis B: comparison between liver biopsy and elastometry (Fibroscan). J. Afr. Hepatol. Gastroenterol. 2016; 10 (3):132-137.

4. European Association for the Study of the Liver. EASL clinical practice guidelines on the management of hepatitis B virus infection. J Hepatol. 2017; 67(2):370-398.

5. EASL-ALEH Clinical Practice Guidelines: Non-invasive tests for evaluation of liver disease severity and prognosis. J Hepatol. 2015; 63(1):237-64.

6. Wai CT, Greenson JK, Fontana RJ, Kalbfleisch JD, Marrero JA, Conjeevaram HS et al. A simple non invasive index can predict both significant fibrosis and cirrhosis in patients with chronic hepatitis C. Hepatology. 2003; 38 : 518-26.

7. Sterling RK, Lissen E, Clumeck N, Sola R, Correa MC, Montaner J et al. Development of a simple non invasive index to predict significant fibrosis in patients with HIV/HCV co infection. Hepatology. 2006; 43 : 1317-25.

8. Liu DP, Lu W, Zhang ZQ. Comparative evaluation of GPR versus APRI and FIB -4 in predicting different levels of liver fibrosis of chronic hepatitis B. J Viral Hepat. 2018; 25(5): 581–589.

9. Cadranel JF, Rufat P, Degos F. Practices of liverbiopsy in France: results of a prospective nationwidesurvey. For the Group of Epidemiology of the French Association for the Study of the Liver (AFEF). Hepatology. 2000 ; 32(3):477-81.
10. Regev A, Berho M, Jeffers LJ, Milikowski C, Molina EG, Pyrsopoulos NT et al. Sampling error and intraobserver variation in liverbiopsy in patients withchronic HCV infection. The American journal of gastroenterology. 2002 ;97(10):2614-8.
11.Chon YE, Choi EH, Song KJ, Park JY, Kim DY, Han KH et al. Performance of Transient Elastography for the Staging of Liver Fibrosis in Patients with Chronic Hepatitis B: A Meta-Analysis. PLoS ONE 2012; 7(9): e44930.

12. Basar O, Yimaz B, Ekiz F, Ginis Z, Altinbas A, Aktas B, et al. Non-invasive tests in prediction of liverfibrosis in chronichepatitis B and comparisonwith post-antiviral treatmentresults. Clin ResHepatolGastroenterol. 2013;37(2):152–8.
13. Taibi L, Guéchot J. Non-invasive evaluation of hepatic fibrosis. Revue Francophone Des Laboratoires, 2017(491), 38-44.
14. Xiao G, Yang J, Yan L. Comparison of diagnostic accuracy of aspartate aminotransferase to platelet ratio index and fibrosis-4 index for detecting liver fibrosis in adult patients with chronic hepatitis B virus infection: a systemic review and meta-analysis. Hepatology (Baltimore, Md). 2015;61(1):292-302.
15. Mallet V, Dhalluin-Venier V, Roussin C, Bourliere M, Pettinelli ME et al. The accuracy of the FIB-4 index for the diagnosis of mild fibrosis in chronic hepatitis B. Alimentary pharmacology & therapeutics. 2009; 29(4):409-15.
16. Sarin SK, Kumar M, Lau GK, Abbas Z, Chan HL, Chen CJ et al. Asian-Pacific clinical practice guidelines on the management of hepatitis B: a 2015 update. Hepatol Int. 2016; 10 :1-98.

17. World Health Organization. Guidelines for the prevention, care and treatment of persons infected with chronic hepatitis B. 2015.

18. Wai CT, Cheng CL, Wee A, Dan YY, Chan E, Chua W et al. Non-invasive models for predicting histology in patients with chronic hepatitis B. Liver international : official journal of the International Association for the Study of the Liver. 2006;26(6):666-72.

19. Lemoine M, Shimakawa Y, Nayagam S, Khalil M, Suso P, Lloyd J et al. The gamma-glutamyl transpeptidase to platelet ratio (GPR) predicts significant liver fibrosis and cirrhosis in patients withchronic in West Africa. Gut. 2016 ; 65:1369-76.

20. Lian MJ, Zhang JQ, Chen SD, Zhang DD, Yang YY, Hong GL. Diagnostic accuracy of γ-glutamyl transpeptidase-to-platelet ratio for predicting hepatitis B-related fibrosis: a meta-analysis. Eur J GastroenterolHepatol. 2019 ; 31(5):599-606

21. Hu YC, Liu H, Liu XY, Ma LN, Guan YH, Luo X et al. Value of gamma-glutamyltranspeptidase-to-platelet ratio in diagnosis of hepaticfibrosis in patients withchronichepatitis B.World J Gastroenterol. 2017; 23(41): 7425–7432.

22. Degos F, Perez P, Roche B, Mahmoudi A, Asselineau J, Voitot H et al. Diagnostic accuracy of FibroScan and comparison to liver fibrosis biomarkers in chronic viral hepatitis : a multicenter prospective study (the FIBROSTIC study). J Hepatol 2010 ; 53 : 1013-21.

23. Ganne-Carrie N, Ziol M, de Ledinghen V, Douvin C, Marcellin P, Castera L et al. Accuracy of liver stiffness measurement for the diagnosis of cirrhosis in patients with chronic liver diseases. Hepatology 2006 ; 44 : 1511-7.

24. Li Q, Lu C, Li W, Huang Y, Chen L. Impact of age on the diagnostic performances and cut-offs of APRI and FIB-4 for significant fibrosis and cirrhosis in chronic hepatitis B.Oncotarget. 2017; 8(28):45768-45776.

25. Wang L, Fan YX, Dou XG. Declining diagnostic accuracy of non-invasive fibrosis tests is associated with elevated alanine aminotransferase in chronic hepatitis B.World J Clin Cases. 2018; 6(12):521-530.

Abstract

Introduction:

The assessment of the severity of liver damage determines the prognosis and therapeutic indications in chronic hepatitis B. Liver biopsy is currently considered to be the gold standard for assessing the extent of fibrosis and inflammation, however it has certain limitations. Many non-invasive methods are now widely available and are increasingly being implemented in routine clinical practice.

Objective:

To evaluate and compare the diagnostic performances of pulse elastometry (EI), FIB4, APRI and GPR to predict significant fibrosis during chronic hepatitis B in a Tunisian population.

Methods :

Analytical prospective study, spread over a period of 3 years from January 2015 to December 2017, carried out at the gastroenterology department of the Sahloul University Hospital Centre in Sousse on patients followed for chronic hepatitis B. FIB4, APRI and GPR scores were calculated and the AE performed in all patients. The diagnostic performance of the different fibrosis markers was analysed using the Pearson correlation test and the receiver operating curve (ROC) to compare them. The diagnostic values of the scores were calculated using the usual informational indices: sensitivity, specificity, positive (PPV) and negative (NPV) predictive values and areas under the curve (AUROCs).

Results:

A total of 43 patients were included. The mean age was 38 years with a sex ratio M/F= 1.1. Cytolysis was found in 9 patients (20.9%). According to the Metavir score, 30 patients had absent or minimal fibrosis, 13 patients had significant fibrosis and 3 patients had severe fibrosis.

AEs and FIB4 were correlated with significant fibrosis (p=0.001 and 0.04 respectively) with AUROCs of 0.76 and 0.74 respectively.

For a threshold of 6.5 KPa, the AR had the best sensitivity (76%). For a threshold of 1.45, FIB 4 had the best specificity (83.3%). These 2 methods had the best NPVs (83.3%). The AE and FIB4 would thus avoid liver biopsies in 35 (81.3%) and 33 (76.7%) patients respectively. APRI score and GPR were not good markers to predict significant fibrosis with AUROC at 0.58 and 0.54 respectively. Using a cut-off of 0.5 for the APRI score and 0.32 for the GPR, these markers had a low PPV 35% and 32.3% respectively. They prevented liver biopsies in 55.8% and 41.8% of patients respectively.

Conclusion:

In our study population, the AE and FIB4 appear to be reliable for the detection of significant hepatic fibrosis in chronic viral hepatitis B.

Key words :

Chronic viral hepatitis B, non-invasive markers, liver fibrosis, Tunsian population.

Abstract

Background

Fibrosisstagingdetermines the prognosis and therapeutic indications in chronichepatitis B. Liverbiopsywasconsideredto bethe gold standard for assessing the extent of fibrosis and inflammation, but has certaines limitations. Many non-invasive methods are currentlywidelyavailable and increasinglyimplanted in currentclinical practice.

Aim

The aim of ourstudywas to evaluate and compare the diagnostic performance of fibroscan, FIB4, APRI and GPR to predictsignificantfibrosisduringchronichepatitis B in a Tunisian population.

Methods

This was a prospective study, over a period of 3 yearsfromJanuary 2015 to December 2017, conducted in the gastroenterologydepartment of the SahloulUniversity Hospital, on patients followed for chronichepatitis B. The scores APRI, FIB4, GPR werecalcultaed and Transient elastographywereperformed on all patients.

The diagnostic performance of each of the fibrosis markers wasanalyzedusing the Pearson correlation test and the receiver operating curve (ROC) to compare them.

The diagnostic values of the scores werecalculatedusing the usualinformationalindices:sensitivity, specificity, positive predictive (PPV) and negative (NPV) values and areas under the curve (AUROCs).

Results

In total, 43 patients wereincluded. The meanagewas 38 yearswith a sex ratio H / F = 1.1. Cytolysiswasfoundin 20.9% of patients. According to the Metavir score, 30 patients had absent or minimal fibrosis, 13 patients hadsignificantfibrosis and 3 patients hadseverefibrosis.

Fibroscan and FIB4 werecorrelatedwithsignificantfibrosis ($p = 0.001$ and 0.04 respectively) and appeared to be reliable for the detection of significantfibrosis (AUROC of 0.76 and 0.74 respectively).

For a threshold of 6.5 KPa, fibroscan had the best sensitivity (76%). For a threshold of 1.45, FIB 4 had the best specificity (83.3%). These 2 methodshad the best NPV (83.3%). Fibroscan and FIB4 wouldavoidliver biopsies in35 (81.3%) and 33(76.7%) patients respectively.

The APRI score and GPR were not good markers for predictingsignificantfibrosis (AUROC at 0.58 and 0.54, respectively). Using a cut-off of 0.5 for the APRI score and 0.32 for the GPR, these markers had a low PPV (35% and 32.3% respectively). However, theywouldavoidliver biopsies in 55.8% and 41.8% of patients respectively.

Conclusion

In ourstudy population, the fibroscan and FIB4 appear to be reliable for the detection of significantliverfibrosis in chronichepatitis B.

Key-Words

Chronichepatitis B, non-invasive markers, liverfibrosis, tunisian population